The Little Book of Golfing Verse

Mike Wenham

Copyright © Mike Wenham 2004

All rights reserved

No part of this publication may be reproduced, stored in a retrieval system, or transmitted, in any form or by any means electronic, photocopying, recording or otherwise, without the permission of the author

First published in Great Britain by
Pen Press Publishers Ltd
39–41, North Road
Islington
London N7 9DP

ISBN 1-904754-79-1

Cover design Jacqueline Abromeit

Printed and bound in the UK

Acknowledgements

I would like to express my thanks to all members of Worthing Golf Club, some of whom have given me the inspiration to write this book. Particular thanks to:

Tony "Odd Socks" Clark
Richard "Front Foot" Culling
Peter "George" Feltham
Brian "The Knee" Pannell
John "Pavarotti" Polwin
Tony "OJ" Simpson
William "Two Windows" Tyler

Various other Worthing members have been mentioned in verse throughout the book and I sincerely hope that I have not offended them in any way.

Main photo on front cover by Brian Pannell.
All other cover photographs by William Tyler.

Images by "Clip Art"

To; David & Sheila.

Thank you for supporting us this evening.

Best Wishes

Mike W.
Dec 04

Dedications

To Audrey,
my partner in love and golf,
for giving me so much support
and encouragement during
the writing of this book

To Dorothy, the Secretary of the
Southwick Underwater Knitting Club.
Your support is very much appreciated:
I'm wearing it every day.

To Pippa

Golf is a very hygienic game.

What other sport would give you eighteen chances to clean your balls in soapy water?

Contents

It makes you mad	1
Sticking Together	2
GOLF JOKE	3
A Hole in One	4
The Wednesday Four-ball	6
Bandits	8
Buggies	10
In the Bunker	11
Entering the Vets	13
The little shed on the Sixth	14
Representing the Club	16
Where's Old Tom?	17
Slow Play	18
Playing with your Wife	20
They signed my Cap!	22
The Fat Controller	24
Preferred Lies	25
It never rains on a Golf Course	26
GOLF JOKE	28
Medals	29
A New Putter	30
Playing with the Vets	33
Remember Tom?	34
Lost and Found	36
Worst Greens in the County	37
A Golfing Break in Dorset	39
The Saga of Brian's Knee	41
Balls	43
What's in the Flask?	44
Playing through	45
It's in the Bag!	47
GOLF JOKE	49
Swinging Club	50

It makes you mad

Some days it makes you angry.
Some days it makes you glad.
But most of all this game of golf
it makes you blooming MAD.

Upon the tee, your hopes are high
the contact sounded good.
You watch the ball fly high and true
into the nearby wood.

You stand upon the fairway
and swing your trusty wedge.
The ball it takes a wicked slice
and now it's in a hedge.

You take a drop, you make the green,
you've got the putt lined up.
But can you get that little ball
into that great big cup?

And so it goes from bad to worse,
you finally make an eight.
"Never mind," you tell yourself,
"I'll hit the next one straight."

The ball this time does what it's told.
Your drive is long and true.
The iron shot is just as good,
and you're on the green in two.

Twelve feet left, a downhill putt.
You line it up with glee.
A super strike, the ball drops in…
You made a BIRDIE three!

Sticking Together

Mike and Tony, they both play
in a slightly different way
"Back to front" some folk will say,
but Lefthanders stick together.

Pros will recommend a change
Take them to the driving range
Suggest their swing is "very strange"
but Lefthanders stick together.

On the course they do their best
Very often beat the rest
"Most peculiar" some just jest
but Lefthanders stick together.

On the tee, the others look
Tell us we're not by the book
We tell them "we never hook"
cos Lefthanders stick together.

The strangest action ever seen
hit balls from fairways to the green
to places "rights" have never been
Lefthanders stick together.

Golf is such a funny game
You can forget your partner's name
But on the course we're just the same
Lefthanders stick together.

A group of golfers were on the fairway when a funeral cortège passed close by. One of the golfers stopped play, removed his cap and bowed his head. His playing partner complimented him on showing such respect. "It was the least I could do," said the golfer. "We've been married for over thirty years".

A Hole in One

The seventh hole is next to play,
a very tricky long par three.
Players clear the green ahead
and Peter Feltham's on the tee.

Up to now he's had no luck
his handicap is looking frail.
The drives were poor, the chips not good
He's tried his best, to no avail.

Now's the time to make amends
He's feeling pretty good.
"I think I'll take my four iron here
and leave alone my wood."

The swing was as it should have been
The shot was right on line;
The ball pitched nicely on the green,
his best for quite some time.

"But where's the ball?" his partner cried
"It must be near the pin!"
"Off the back" was Peters thought
Surely it can't be in?

Up to the green with hopes held high
the players took a stroll.
And sure enough when they arrived…
Pete's ball was in the HOLE.

The Wednesday Four-ball

It's Wednesday morning, half past ten,
the weather's fine, but cloudy.
The Car Park's filling up at speed
and the Clubroom's getting rowdy.

Bill has got the start sheet out
The player's mill around.
Now's the time to take the plunge
It only costs a pound.

Early starters get in first
Cos sometimes by request
Bill will oblige by getting you
out before the rest.

"First Four" silences the crowd
as we wait to hear our fate.
"Number two and twenty-one
will play with twelve and eight."

The names are called and out you go
but once upon the tee.
You find one player's not arrived,
and now you're down to three.

Bill insists, you must be prompt,
especially early starters.
If you're not ready on the dot,
he'll have your guts for garters.

Back in the club the draw goes on
and more groups join the fray.
At half eleven it looks as though
there could be sixty out today.

Play continues on the course
and fast approaching three.
Players gather in the club
to have their cake and tea.

As others wander in they ask,
"Had a good score today?"
"Not bad, not bad" is your retort.
You give nothing away.

Having played quite well together,
you've scored a forty-five.
Nobody else has mentioned more
and your chances stay alive.

But when the final scores come in
your hopes are not the same.
The winning pair got fifty-one
and you're not in the frame.

But in the end it doesn't matter
if you lose or win.
If you get beaten on the day,
you take it on the chin.

The taking part is what's important;
playing with the "guys"
In seven days' time you all come back
trying to win that prize.

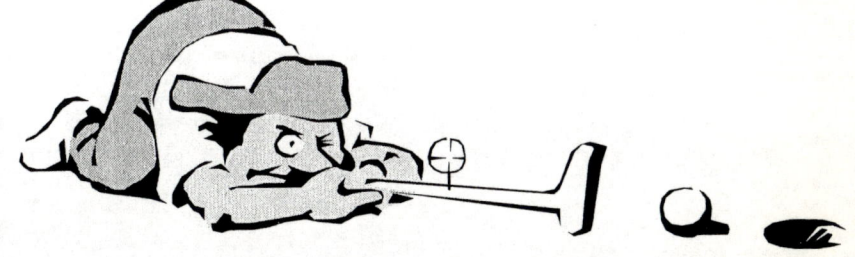

Bandits

If you play golf, you'll know the type of person I describe.
In fact they seem to emanate from one particular tribe.
Every golf club gets them, and Societies pick them up,
and the most annoying factor is they usually win a Cup.

They often join from other clubs – find you in Yellow Pages.
And on the form they indicate they haven't played for ages.
"Why not join us?" you ask the chap, "Have you played before?"
"Not for years, my handicap is twenty-three point four."

The group stood on the opening tee and everyone shook hands.
The "new boy" introduced himself and said his name was Hans.
"I'm not much good," he tells the rest while teeing up his Top Flight
A glorious swing and follow through – the ball is out of sight.

"A lucky shot," he then declares as others watched in awe,
"I've never hit a tee shot quite as far as that before."
His second shot is straight and true, the best they'd ever seen,
The ball takes "back spin" as it lands upon the distant green.

As Hans stood over his three-foot putt, the others had to smile.
If this bloke plays off twenty-three he'd beat them by a mile.
Sure enough the putt dropped in, he scored a three for four
The others hoped that this was luck and soon he'd fail to score.

On he went around the course, in pars and birdies too.
The worst score he had half way round was a lucky six for two.
He kept on saying "beginners luck" as he stacked up the pars.
"If this blokes not a bandit, Tom, then I'm the King of Mars."

The round is over, Hans has won with forty-seven points.
The other players curse their luck and rub their aching joints.
"Are you playing with us next week, Hans, in the Stableford?"
"Oh no," he says," I don't play Comps – I'm really not that good."

And now you know just what we mean by "Bandits" on the course.
The only thing that's missing is their lovely piebald horse.
They play in friendlies, use their shots, and usually take the money.
But never play in qualifiers – now don't you think that's funny?

Buggies

The thing that gets me quite uptight
and often drives me barmy
Is when you're playing on the course
in front of the "Buggie Army".

You're just about to play your shot,
when suddenly you find
To your dismay you look to see
two buggies close behind.

Why do they have to push so hard?
Why can't they blinking wait?
When they keep rushing up behind
they get me in a state.

I realise that when you're old
you find it difficult walking.
But when they push right up your back
they're practically stalking!

Perhaps I'm being rather harsh
and ought to be more mellow.
The next time they are on my tail,
I promise I won't bellow.

At the moment, I can walk
and shouldn't get so miffed.
but in the future, you never know
I might need a lift!

In the Bunker

You've seen Pros on the telly when their ball goes in the sand,
They line it up just left of pin, their wedges in their hand.
They swing their club through smoothly, making sure they don't look up,
And if by magic, that little ball ends two feet from the cup.

"I can do that," you declare, as you face your bunker shot.
You take your stance, adjust your feet, and give it all you've got.
A spray of sand, a great big hole, shows where you're ball had been,
And then you find it's in the trap on the other side of the green.

You skulk across as others wait and re-address the ball.
This time you get the blighter out; you're feeling six foot tall.
But wait a bit, it's rolling fast through green and over brow,
Right into the very bunker that you were in just now!

Back across the green you go, the others glance away,
They're hoping that your ball comes out, before their hair goes grey.
The group behind are waiting now, and someone's shouting "fore",
You start to think that you're not keen on playing any more.

The lie this time is not so good, it's up against the bank,
Your playing partner's taking bets you'll end up with a shank.
But what the heck, you blast it out, and when the sand mist clears,
Everybody on the green is very close to tears.

"Where did it go?" you ask the guys, as they all roll about,
The group behind are jumping around, and they begin to shout.
Your partner dries his eyes and wanders over to the pole,
And sure enough your little ball is nestled in the hole!

Entering the Vets

The players gather in the club
and all becomes quite clear.
The entry forms are on the board
for the Veterans games this year.

To be a Vet you need to be
some sixty years of age.
And often over thirty names
appear on every page.

The room is crowded out today.
You push to get a space.
You enter then for every match
and hope you get a place.

As weeks go by, the notices
are gradually taken down.
This means the Secretary must
have donned his cap and gown.

Before too long the teams are picked
and everyone can see
just who they will be playing with
and where the match will be.

"Not him again" you tell yourself,
"Oh, no – it can't be true."
But don't forget, he probably thinks
the same thing about you!

And most of all you should be glad
you actually get some games.
Some of us are **Fifty-Five**
and can't put down our names!

The little shed on the Sixth

You hear a lot of golfing tales,
and some of them are true.
But here is one that I was told…
I'll pass it on to you.

Two friends met one hot summer's morn,
some holes of golf to play.
They started out with spirits high,
Looked forward to their day.

They noticed as they played the first
that up upon the green.
A man and girl were putting out,
it seemed a pleasant scene.

The first three holes were halved in par
but when they got to four
They spotted that the pair in front
were visible no more.

They played the fifth, again a half,
and wandered to the tee.
A long par five awaited them,
the sixth green they could see.

"They moved on quick," one golfer said.
"The hole's completely clear."
But then he was quite taken back
at what he soon would hear.

From just behind the tee there came,
a shriek and then a moan.
They turned around and both could see
that they were on their own.

"What was that?" Bill asked his friend.
"I don't know," answered Fred.
He pointed back behind the tee,
"It came from in that shed."

They dropped their clubs and wandered back
The moans came more and more.
They reached the shed, and poked their heads
around the open door.

The sight they saw gave them a start
they'd found the missing pair.
The man was looking rather flushed,
and the girl was almost bare.

Bill and Fred stood open mouthed,
They didn't know what to do.
Then Bill spoke those immortal words…
"Mind if we play through?"

Representing the Club

Some time ago, upon the board
a notice caught my eye.
It asked for names to play a match
against a club nearby.
"Why not," I thought and very soon
my name was on the list.
To represent my club at golf,
a chance not to be missed.

Within a week the team was picked
and much to my surprise,
My name was there upon that list,
I couldn't believe my eyes!
I told my mates, I told my Mum,
I had to tell my wife.
I couldn't wait for my big day,
the proudest of my life.

At last the morning of the match
arrived, and I was ready.
I packed my kit, cleaned up my clubs,
and tried my nerves to steady.
I reached the club with time to spare
and waited for the rest.
Checked my get-up in the mirror,
I had to look my best.

The changing room was very quiet,
and so I ventured out.
To see if any of my team
were wandering about.
But not a soul was there to see
except my lonely car.
So back inside I quickly strode
and went up to the Bar.

I asked the steward "Are they here?"
And then he ruined my day.
"I think, my friend, you've got it wrong,
"The team are playing AWAY"

Where's Old Tom?

We had a bloke who joined the club a couple of years ago.
His name was Tom; he came from Wales, and often told you so!
We never knew how old he was, but he was past his prime
and he turned up almost every day, just to pass the time.

"Feel free to join us," someone said, and sure enough he came.
He joined the Wednesday Four-ball and looked forward to his game.
People showed him where to put his name upon the list,
It seemed to take a little while for him to get the gist.

The problem was he didn't know that once you're on the sheet.
You must make sure that you have got your golf shoes on your feet.
If Uncle Bill draws out the groups, and it's your name he calls,
Rest assured, if you're not there, he'll have you by the balls.

And sure enough, Tom's name came out, and he was duly missing.
Bill was calling "Where is he?" and soon he started hissing.
He stormed into the clubroom where old Tom was supping tea,
and then politely told him he should join the other three.

Old Tom jumped up and quickly joined his partners on the Tee.
"I'm sorry, chaps," he blurted out, apologetically.
He told them that old Bill had knocked the wind out of his sails
But all agreed it served him right – remember, he's from WALES!

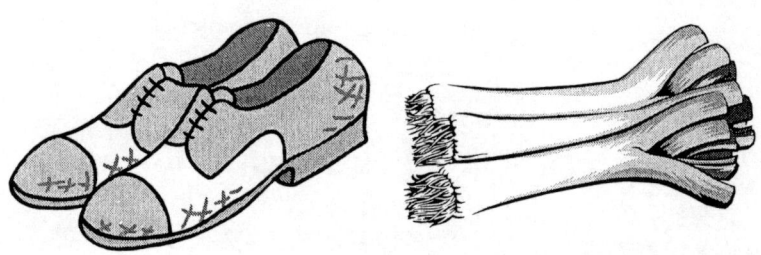

Slow Play

The draw is made and in your four
you have a player who
is very slow to take his shots;
Think on, it could be you!

You'll know him when he puts his ball
upon the teeing ground.
Takes one step back, then walks away
and starts to wander round.

A practice swing or two will follow,
and then he stares ahead.
He finally walks up to the ball
as you start to shake your head.

Another swing will follow now,
before the ball's addressed.
By this time all the other lads
are getting very stressed.

It looks as though he's nearly ready,
and finally he swings.
By now you've all lost interest,
and think of other things.

At last his ball is on its way,
You punch the air with glee.
But then you turn around and find
there's two groups on the tee.

Perhaps he's quicker on the green,
the thought will cross your mind,
if he's not, we'll all get slated
by the group behind.

It's his turn now to take his putt
He places down his ball.
Then he walks ten paces back
and starts to survey all.

The line, the slope, the speed of stroke,
it all goes through his mind.
And all you lads can think about
is the baying mob behind.

He's walking back up to the ball,
He's quickening his stride.
Wait a minute, now he's looking
from the other side!

At last he's ready at the ball,
It'll soon be on its way.
But, no, it's three more practice strokes
before he's ready to play.

The group behind are pulling hair.
There's twelve of them in all.
They start to sing in unison,
"HIT THE BLOODY BALL"

With all that noise, the putt is missed,
It's four feet past the hole.
You all insist he can't repeat
the previous rigmarole.

Oh, yes he can, and sure enough
he goes through his routine.
You look behind, and no surprise.
The mob is now sixteen.

He finally putts, goes six feet past,
and looks across at Jimmy.
"Pick it up," says Jim at once,
"That's definitely a Gimme."

Playing with your Wife

There comes a time in a golfer's life
when he starts playing with his wife.
She's watched him leave the house each day,
and always asks him, "Can I play?"

She had some lessons on the range,
At first she found it rather strange.
But very soon the swing was better,
She followed guidance to the letter.

"I think you're ready," said the Pro,
"Get on the course; give it a go."
Soon the fateful match was fixed
You're entered in the Evening Mixed.

What will all your mates be saying,
when they find your wife is playing.
Will she make you feel a fool?
Will she understand each rule?

And so at last the big day came
and she was ready for the game.
And as you stood upon the tee
you pulled her over; "Listen to me."

"When we get out on the course,
remember, I'm the driving force.
I will tell you how you play,
and make sure that it stays that way."

She looks at you, a face like thunder.
You realise you've made a blunder.
She spits from under her bobble hat,
"Don't you talk to me like that."

From this point on the air is tense,
You should have known she'd take offence.
So now you try to make amends,
"I'm sorry dear – can we be friends?"

With damage done, you're in the poo.
She doesn't want to talk to you.
You realise you are the sinner,
There's going to be a silent dinner.

Your wife is playing to the letter,
sinking putts and playing better.
You are getting gradually worse,
since you got the dreaded curse.

At the end, the match is won.
And knowing something must be done
you tell her, "Darling, may I say,
you played very well today."

If looks could kill, you'd drop down dead.
She gives a sigh, and turns her head.
"Thank you dear, and may I say,
you played like a twit today."

They signed my Cap!

Last year we went to Tenerife for seven days of sun,
and we were looking forward to some golf as well as fun.
We saw a great big notice on the wall of our abode
that the Canarias Open was being held just up the road.

Now we had never seen the pros in action, not at all,
so we grabbed the hotel telephone and quickly made a call.
"How much to watch?" I asked the bloke. He told me ten Euro,
and we thought it was a bargain so we'd definitely go.

We found the course at Adeje, not fifteen miles away,
and then we learnt our local lad had made the final day.
We checked the list, and sure enough young Gary made the cut.
We pushed our way right through the crowd and found the starters' hut.

Up on the tee was Phillip Price, a tallish chap from Wales,
His tee shot went three hundred yards – the wind was in his sails.
Alongside him was Sergio, an unknown Spanish bloke,
He rattled off a longer one – that made our Phillip choke.

The group moved off with quite a crowd, about three hundred strong,
Which left just Audrey and myself; we hadn't been there long.
Onto the tee the next group came, and it was no surprise,
to see our hero Gary Evans right before our eyes.

The other two in Gary's group we cannot quite recall,
but one of them from Argentina really whacked the ball.
His tee shot flew right out of sight, and Gary did the same.
It really was a great big thrill to see him on his game.

We followed him around the course and watched his every shot.
We saw him drive, we saw him chip, we watched him sink the lot.
The crowds ahead were very noisy, following Serg and Phil,
but apart from me and Audrey, Gary's gallery was NIL.

It didn't matter, we would clap, as Gary sunk his putts.
He got the birdies, eagles too; he really had the guts.
He reached the last just off the lead at nine shots under par.
By now the TV camera crew were following by car.

And down the last, a long par five, he made a birdie four.
That final day had seen our Gary almost win on tour.
And as he shook his partner's hand he turned to look our way
and nodded his approval for supporting him that day.

He walked towards the official tent to register his score,
Then we saw him beckon us as he came out the door.
Right next to him was Sergio, that little Spanish chap.
And both of them got out a pen and signed my golfing cap!

It made my day; I went all silly. Audrey told me straight,
"Stop behaving like a child; you're nearly fifty-eight."
But she will never understand it gave me such a thrill,
and that signed cap sits proudly on my office window sill.

The Fat Controller

Chaps who play with me will know,
that I don't use a driver.
Come to think of it, I can't
hit a three wood either.

God knows, I've tried. I did my best
when Arnie gave me tips.
But every time I sliced the ball,
a curse would pass my lips.

"Eye on the ball," he'd say to me
"Keep your head right down."
And as the ball pinged to the left
his face would start to frown.

I must admit, he did persist,
But then we both agreed.
"Forget the woods; it's certainly,
a driving iron you need."

The "controller" is the club I use
when standing on the Tee.
And rest assured, I drive as far
as the blokes who play with me.

As I play my golf each week
and prepare to take my drive
I think, "I can't be all that bad,
I play off eleven point five."

Preferred Lies

A player stood above his ball that nestled in the rough.
He realised that getting it out was going to be quite tough.
His opponent stood across the fairway in a super spot,
pondering which club to use for his forthcoming shot.

The player with the tricky one then noticed with delight,
his mate wanted a comfort stop and scuttled out of sight.
He took the opportunity to bend down to his ball,
and pick it up to drop it where there was no rough at all.

He picked a club, took his shot, and plopped it on the green.
Just as his opponent ventured out from where he'd been.
"Wait a minute, you were in the rough just over there.
You moved the ball, you cheated," he ventured to declare.

"Not strictly true," the man retorted, staring at his eyes.
"Don't forget that in this weather we play preferred lies."
"Not in the rough," his mate replied, "I really think you've erred."
"Ah, but the place I played from was the lie that I preferred."

It never rains on a Golf Course

The alarm goes off at half past seven,
you slide out of your bed,
and drawing back the curtains
you start to scratch your head.

You rub your eyes and stare outside,
and have to look again.
It can't be true, it isn't fair,
it's pouring hard with rain.

Now just last night the forecast said
that rain would clear by dawn.
The sun would shine and just
a short-sleeved T-shirt could be worn.

You're playing golf today, you see;
the weather must be good.
It's been some time since you have swung,
an iron or a wood.

A wash and shave, and soon you're ready
to pack your golfing kit.
You glance outside to check the rain,
and think it's eased a bit.

Once in the car you are convinced,
the rain will clear away.
You'll be keeping fingers crossed,
that the course is fit for play.

You near the club, but now it seems
the rain is getting worse.
"Just my luck" you tell yourself,
trying not to curse.

As you drive in, you're pleased to see
the course is fit for play.
You hope the clouds will thin quite soon,
and really make your day.

In the clubhouse friends await,
and what is this you're hearing.
Out to the west there's clear blue sky;
the weather's duly clearing.

So at last the sun comes out,
and the clouds have blown away.
Was there really any doubt,
that you would play today?

A match was in progress and one golfer in particular was having trouble with his putting. Every time he missed the hole he would let out a curse "Bugger it, missed." A lady golfer in the group was getting upset and asked him not to use such language on the course. Two holes later the same thing; he missed his putt and shouted, "Bugger it, missed." Once again the lady warned him, and being a religious person she told him that if he did it again she would ask God to send a bolt of lightning down on to his head. At the next hole the trend continued and as his putt slid past the hole he wailed, "Bugger it, missed." The sky darkened at once and a huge bolt of lightning flashed down to earth and struck the lady golfer on the head, knocking her to the ground. A voice boomed from the heavens above... "Bugger it, missed."

Medals

Most golfers will tell you, there's one thing they dread,
The thing that they just can't get into their head,
The match that they think about, two weeks ahead…
They don't want to play in the Medal.

Four-balls and Stableford; these are both fine.
Match play and friendlies you play all the time.
But the thing that will always get golfers to whine..
is having to play in the Medal.

It's pressure you see, counting all of those shots,
Thinking about it ties your stomach in knots.
You'll finish up playing from nasty old spots…
if you sign up to play in the Medal.

In Stableford format there's no fuss at all
If you're out of shots you just pick up your ball.
But one sort of golf leads to many a fall…
you've guessed it, that nasty old Medal.

Three off the tee, and lost balls in the rough,
Twelve over par after four holes is tough,
And shortly you're thinking that you've had enough…
of playing in this blooming Medal.

You hack you're way round, losing heart as you go,
Waiting on shots makes your progress so slow.
In the back of your mind there is one thing you know…
You'll no longer play in the Medal!

A New Putter

Perhaps a new putter
will lower your score.
The one you've been using,
doesn't work any more.
But which one to choose
is the problem you face.
They change the designs
at a frightening pace.

There's long ones and short ones,
they both have their charms.
Some fit in your belly
or under your arms.
Some have got bends in
and some are just straight,
with lumps on the end
to increase the weight.

The head of the putter
is now setting a trend,
with two or three golf balls
stuck on the end.
There's one now that looks
like it's out of Star Trek
You're beginning to think
it's a pain in the neck.

Inside the golf shop
you look at the stacks
of putters all lined up
on neat little racks.
You need to decide
on one that you like.
And try some to get a
good feel of the strike.

Twenty-five minutes
of testing pass by.
But none of the putters
appeal to the eye.
Then all of a sudden,
almost hidden from view,
you notice one strangely
familiar to you.

On that little mat that
they have in the shop.
You try it and soon find
the balls start to drop,
The weight is just perfect,
it really feels great.
You're sinking the putts
at a frightening rate.

"I'll take it," you say
to the lad at the till.
As you get out money
to settle the bill.
"Have it for nothing,"
said the lad with a grin.
"This is the putter,
that you've just brought in!"

And so there's a moral
to this little rhyme.
Don't blame your putter
for missing each time.
There's some other reason
you're missing the cup.
It must be the way
that your lining it up!

Playing with the Vets

You have to be sixty to play in the team
to visit those golf clubs where you've never been.
Eat lovely meals, drinking wine... Oh it's mean,
I wish I could play with the Vets.

They come back from matches with plenty to say
about birdies and bogies and excellent play.
They talk about how it was such a great day...
Oh, I wish I could play with the Vets.

There's Mannings Heath, Bognor, East Brighton as well.
Goodwood and Cowdray come under their spell.
There's plenty of stories their willing to tell...
How I wish I could play with the Vets.

The captains make speeches just after the lunch.
They tell a few stories as dinner they munch,
then offer the team members plenty of punch...
Oh, I wish I could play with the Vets.

The problem you see is that I'm not that old
Us young ones are frequently left in the cold.
I really would like to be called to the fold...
I just wish I could play with the Vets.

My mates play in most games, travelling around,
Much thought I have given, and suddenly found,
when I'm old enough, they'll be under the ground...
So I don't want to play in the Vets.

Remember Tom?

Old Tom Blewis came from Wales,
we told you earlier on.
But now we got some urgent news,
we're not too sure he's gone!

When he was here he drove us mad,
with jokes that weren't that good.
We tried to slip away at times,
but follow us he would.

He'd tell us stories about his life,
he really was a bore.
And worst of all he'd told the tales
twenty times before!

On Wednesdays we would ask of others
"Is old Tom Blewis about?"
If he was, we wouldn't enter
until he'd been called out.

Alas, old Tom went back to Wales,
We couldn't share a joke.
And do you know, it pains to say…
I really missed the bloke.

But has he gone, we ask ourselves,
as just the other day.
We all walked off the 18th green
and who stood in our way?

It is… it's him! He's back again,
we can't believe our eyes.
I hide behind the nearest tree,
and Tony Simpson sighs.

And there he was, the man from Wales.
Tom Blewis in his glory.
The others made a dash for it,
before he told a story.

I took his hand and shook it hard,
and asked him with a grin.
"How are you Tom, you old Welsh twit."
He took it on the chin.

We talked a while and then he asked,
if we could share a jar.
"A good idea" we both agreed,
and wandered to the Bar.

As we walked in the room was packed,
from ceiling down to floor.
But when they saw old Tom walk in,
they all ran out the door!

Old Tom was really there that day,
I wouldn't tell you tales.
And now he's back where he belongs…
in his beloved WALES.

Lost and Found

When I'm in the Locker Room,
I have a look around.
To see the things that people leave,
in the section "Lost and Found".

I find it strange that there is oft
a single shoe in there.
When they're driving home at night
I wonder what they wear?

You sometimes see a single sock,
left lying on the floor.
Next to a pair of underpants
not wanted any more.

Belts and caps and bobble hats
are very often found.
Dirty towels and soggy jumpers
lie upon the ground.

Club head covers, dirty hankies,
a pair of fishnet tights?
If they find the bloke who left them there,
He should be read his rights!

So, next time you are at the club.
Just have a look yourself.
And see what sort of junk gets left
up on that old top shelf.

Worst Greens in the County

Anytown Golf Club, half past ten,
the lads are on the tee.
There's seven of us, that's OK,
we'll play a four and three.

But wait a minute, we can't go yet.
There's something very wrong.
Richard's still in the car park
putting his wet gear on.

At last we start, two groups of four.
And we're all full of beans.
But it isn't long before our Dick
is running down the greens.

"Just look at this, no grass at all,"
he mutters on the third.
"I played at Ham the other week –
their greens are quite superb."

We battle on and tell him straight,
each time he has a moan.
He'll have to pay a little fine
before he ventures home.

"Worst greens in Sussex," he declares.
That cost him another pound.
At this rate he will be quite skint
by the time we finish the round.

"I've heard a rumour," Richard says.
"If members have their say,
and the greens aren't right by mid July
there's changes on the way."

We soldier on, he moans at will,
"These greens are getting worse."
But we don't mind, his little fines
are filling up the purse.

At last we reach the eighteenth green
Richard stands over his ball.
He strokes it in for a birdie three,
and the greens are OK after all!

A Golfing Break in Dorset

It's right next door to Monkey World, just up the road from Bere.
The Dorset Golf and Country Club, we went down there last year.
A four-day break and lots of golf was what we had in store,
and certainly we weren't let down - in fact we wanted more.

Eight of us were in the squad and six had been before.
John and Peter joined us, to make two teams of four.
Rooms were sorted, luggage dumped, and soon we're on the tee.
Mike has brought his camera down to make a short movie.

The course is great, weather fine, and soon we're in the points.
We find that using Buggies helps the old boy's aching joints.
Those that came the year before have knowledge of the course,
but both the new boys find it hard to be a potent force.

As day one ends the leader board is looking very tight.
It's nice to see that everyone is keen to join the fight.
Brian, John and lefty Mike are heading up the table,
and just behind is holder William, ready, fit and able.

The evening meal is most delightful, and everyone agrees
the Bar is just the very place to put us all at ease.
Later on it's Brian's quiz that keeps us on our toes,
but good old Johnny Polwin prefers to have a doze.

We all decide the time has come to teach old Clarkie pool,
and it's not long before he proves that he is not a fool.
"He's played before," says Tony S, with a smile upon his face.
Willy Tyler gives a wink: "I'll put him in his place."

The bar is shut, it's time for bed, and Brian wakes up John.
They share a room and he insists he keeps his trousers on.
William "T" and Tony "S" will have a late-night tipple.
Richard Culling does his press-ups – watch his muscles ripple!

Mike has orders from Brenda Clark, and has a plan to hatch.
He must ensure that Tony has a pair of socks that match.
so he picks a pair of white and lays them out upon the bed.
Half way round the course next day, he finds that one is red!

The second day is like the first and everyone plays well.
But who is pushing for the Cup, it's very hard to tell.
Brian and John both find it tough, and William's falling back,
It looks as though young Peter is keeping it on track.

Tony's ball is in a bunker, Richard's found the rough.
Peter rolled into a ditch and found the going tough.
William's air shot was his first and did he feel a pillock.
Tony Clark surveyed it all as he stood on a hillock.

Down the last it's nip and tuck with Mike and Peter duelling.
William's finished, Clarkie's done, and Brian needs refuelling.
Around the green the tension's mounting, just as it should be,
then Peter takes the Dorset Trophy with a birdie three.

And so the week comes to an end, and the prizes are dished out.
We all agree that playing golf is what it's all about.
Next year is booked and everyone will definitely be back,
so thank you Dorset, you deserve a pat upon the back.

The Saga of Brian's Knee

Looking back a year or so, it often came to mind
Why was it that Brian was lagging just behind?
"It looks as though he's knackered," we would sometimes say
And then it dawned upon us the reason for delay.

Some years ago young Brian was a cricketer you know.
Bowling was his forte, and he was never slow.
As he charged towards the wicket, extra pace he found
His knee would jolt quite badly as his front foot hit the ground.

Many years of "leg's before" and lengthy bowling stints
put a strain on knobbly knees and often made him wince.
"Time to stop," he then declared, and thought of other things.
"Golf's the game," he told himself, and bought a set of Pings.

Eagles, Birdies, Bogeys, Pars... all came Brian's way,
Playing golf was just the thing to pass the time of day.
He picked up many trophies, was always in the frame,
It soon became quite obvious that golfing was his game.

Very soon the knees got bad, and started causing pain.
His golf began to worry him and energy to drain.
His Doctor recommended that he have a brand new knee.
"Can I have 'em both done, Doc – Buy One get One Free?"

The "Op" was done, and very soon he came round from the gas
The nursing staff said he'd become a right pain in the...
"I'm very pleased," the Doctor told him. "Go home if you like."
And just to get some exercise he bought himself a bike.

Round the village, up the road, Brian would take his walk.
Every half a dozen yards someone would stop to talk
Finally, he'd had enough; the Golf Club drew him back,
A walk around the lower course will get him back on track.

And so it's done, the knee is fine, and hopefully quite soon
He will be back upon the greens, his putting back in tune.
It looks as though his brand new knee will give him extra length,
And hopefully his golfing skills will go from strength to strength.

Balls

Some golf balls are yellow,
but most come in white.
Some go short distances,
a few "out of sight".

Many are special ones,
giving you spin.
They do what you want,
when attacking the pin.

There's soft ones and hard ones,
and some that feel nice.
Others will promise to
cure that bad slice!

Balls that are cut proof,
with titanium covers.
They all say they travel,
much better than others.

High energy cores,
give you much better feel.
Very confusing,
and almost unreal.

A ball is a ball,
and when you take a swipe.
It goes where you hit it…
Forget all the hype!

What's in the Flask?

Every Monday at seven fifteen,
the group meet for a game.
They play in teams of four or three,
the format's much the same.

Out on the course it gets quite cold,
this early in the day.
You need to keep your body warm,
to help you on your way.

Thermal vests and woolly gloves,
a scarf around the neck.
With all this weight it's hard to get,
the ball up off the deck.

Very soon we're half way round,
now comes the nicest task.
We all unzip our golfing bags,
and reach in for the flask.

Unscrew the cap, and take a sniff
to smell the medicine.
It could be Brandy, maybe Rum,
or something mixed with Gin.

There's just a hint of coffee there,
but not too much to spoil,
the very welcome spirit
that will keep us on the boil.

And so the players soldier on
with warmth back in their souls.
And all at once the bigger balls,
drop into bigger holes!

Playing through

Out on the course the group in front
are holding up the play.
The speed they're moving makes you think,
they won't complete today.

You give a call to gee them up,
but it's totally ignored.
They plod along and now you find,
your getting rather bored.

You have to wait on every hole,
your game has gone to pot.
You watch as Mrs What's-her-name
lines up her umpteenth shot.

"I've had enough," your friend decides,
and squares up to his ball.
He cracks a three wood down the middle,
not bothering to call.

His ball runs through the group in front,
the ladies turn around.
Then one of them lets out a shout,
and throws her club to ground.

She turns and marches down the course,
her arms swing by her side.
She looks as though she's after blood,
the four of you decide.

Her pace increases stride by stride,
and now she's spitting fire.
"What the hell is going on?"
she ventures to enquire.

"Don't you know the rules of golf?"
she yells at your mate Robin.
You notice that her face is red,
and her head has started throbbing.

Robin stood his ground and looked
the lady in the eye.
"You've lost two holes, and in the rules
you must let us pass by."

She stood in front of Robin now,
her hands upon her hips.
And sure enough those telling words,
were soon to pass her lips.

"I don't care if we've lost holes,"
she told him to his face.
"I'm the Lady Captain, and
I play at my own pace."

"But if you want to play on through,
just change your tactics slightly.
We would gladly let you by…
If you just ask politely."

It's in the Bag!

How many times have you looked in your bag
for an item you need in a hurry.
And all you can find is a mishmash of junk
and a smell that reminds you of curry.

The answer of course is to clean out the bag,
so out to the garage you go.
A bin liner ready to hold all the junk,
cos what you will find you don't know.

The first pocket opened contains all your tees,
a couple of gloves and some balls.
But then you discover a sweaty black sock,
a pen, and an old pair of smalls.

The next one reveals some more balls and a tie,
and as you are groping around,
you feel a soft smelly thing down at the bottom,
and wonder what you have just found.

You pull your hand out and give it a sniff,
Banana if you're not mistaken.
Removing it quickly you suddenly find
it's mixed up with some old bits of bacon!

So now you are wary of what you might meet
as you pull down the zip at the back.
But this one's not bad, just a dirty old cap,
which you pull out and drop in the sack.

The next pocket throws up a mixture of things,
some string, rubber bands and a cleat.
But then you make contact with something not nice…
a horribly sticky boiled sweet.

You're getting quite close now to ending the task,
but there's still just one pocket to clear.
You left it till last, as it's stuffed to the top
but you hope that there's nothing to fear.

You cautiously delve down into the abyss,
to feel what is lurking inside.
A pair of wet trousers, an old bobble hat;
the Club sweater you wear with such pride.

Down at the bottom it's getting quite dark,
as you pull out a sock and some gum.
Old scorecards and biros, one leaking its ink,
and some plasters if you cut your thumb.

A bottle of water is next to appear,
and you notice its started to smell.
A few sticky sweets and some mouldy old crisps,
and a half rotten apple as well.

Just as you think that you finished the job,
and there's nothing left inside the bag.
You pull out a soft, squidgy, bundle of stuff
That is wrapped in an old oily rag.

You open it carefully, eager to see,
the treasure that's been tucked away.
And what do you find; it's that nice piece of cake,
that your wife put in last Christmas Day.

The man stood by the seventh green,
his legs were all a quiver.
He gave a cough, his arm fell off,
and floated down the river.*

* The river in question runs behind the seventh green, which is also guarded by a large bunker at the front right. The ideal approach to the green is a right to left draw, bearing in mind that the green is two-tiered, and the upper tier slopes from right to left......Zzzzz_{zzzzz}